AMERICANO

Also by Emanuel Xavier:

Pier Queen
Christ-Like

AMERICANO

emanuel xavier

suspect thoughts press
www.suspectthoughts.com

Some of these poems first appeared, in slightly different versions, in the following newspapers, magazines, journals, and anthologies: *excess compassion, Latin Girl Magazine, LGNY Latino, Lodestar Quarterly, Long Shot, Of The Flesh: Dangerous New Fiction, Poetic Voices, QV Magazine, San Antonio Express-News, and Urban Latino Magazine.*

Cover image and design by Shane Luitjens/Torquere Creative. Book design by Greg Wharton/Suspect Thoughts Press.

ISBN: 0-9710846-2-9

Suspect Thoughts Press
2215-R Market Street, PMB #544
San Francisco, CA 94114-1612
www.suspectthoughts.com

Special thanks and much love to Stephanie Holley,
Craig Roseberry, Dominic Brando, Esther Cuesta,
Jerry Estrella, Mark Doty, and Travis Montez.

Xtra Special thanks to Michael TeVault.

Xtra Xtra Special thanks to
Greg Wharton and Shane Luitjens.

This book is dedicated to my fans.

AMERICANO

contents

WARS AND RUMORS OF WARS

"Ye shall hear of wars and rumors of wars;
see that ye not be troubled;
for all these things must come to pass, but the end is not yet"
-Matthew 24:6

1.
I escape the horrors of war with a towel and a room
Offering myself to Palestinian and Jewish boys
as a 'piece' to the Middle East
when I should be concerned with the untimely deaths
of dark-skinned babies
and the brutal murders of light-skinned fathers

2.
I've been more consumed with how to make
the cover of local fag rags
than how to open the minds of angry little boys
trotting loaded guns
Helpless in finding words that will stop the blood
from spilling like secrets into soil
where great prophets are buried

3.
I return to the same spaces where I once dealt drugs
a celebrated author gliding past velvet ropes
while my club kid friends are mostly dead
from an overdose or HIV-related symptoms
Marilyn wears the crown of thorns
while 4 out of the 5 weapons used to kill Columbine students
had been sold by the same police force that came to their rescue
Not all terrorists have features too foreign
to be recognized in the mirror
Our mistakes are our responsibility

4.
The skyline outside my window
is the only thing that has changed
Men still rape women and blame them for their weaknesses
Children are still molested
by the perversion of Catholic guilt
My boyfriend still takes comfort in the other white powder-
the one used solely to destroy himself and those around him
Not the one used to ignite and create carnage
or mailbox fear

5.
It is said when skin is cut,
and then pressed together, it seals
but what about acid-burned skulls
engraved with the word 'faggot',
a foot bone with flesh and other crushed body parts

6.
It was a gay priest that read last rites
to firefighters as towers collapsed
It was a gay pilot that crashed a plane
into Pennsylvania fields
It was a gay couple that was responsible
for the tribute of light in memory of the fallen
Taliban leaders would bury them to their necks
and tumble walls to crush their heads
Catholic leaders simply condemn them as perverts
having offered nothing but sin
Queer blood is just rosaries scattered on tile

7.
Heroes do not always get heaven

8.
We all have wings... some of us just don't know why

TERESA

I buy my boyfriend's niece Ashley
a Teresa doll for her birthday
Barbie's token Latina friend
a darker skinned replica
which would hopefully teach her multiculturalism
or at least bridge the differences
between her white skinhead-looking uncle and myself

but Teresa doesn't look much like anyone in my *familia*
let alone other Latina's like Shakira, Selena or Eva Peron,
though I'm sure Evita was often compared to Barbie herself
but Teresa doesn't own her own dream house or Corvette
Teresa is rarely found in toy stores as a doctor
or an astronaut or Naval officer
then again, she isn't packaged as a maid
or a factory worker or a mother of five
like my aunts or nieces or cousins
as if there should be shame involved in portraying a Latina doll
as either successful and ambitious or hard-working and real

Teresa's luscious long black hair, slim hips and generic dent
representing the diversities of my culture
is about as practical as Barbie representing all women
I suppose I should be grateful to be acknowledged
as a consumer by Mattel
oft ignored throughout history
Walking down museum aisles
noticing all the statues of gods are white
religions which once dominated culture
until Jesus and Mary were remodeled to look more like Barbie

Ashley takes out her doll collection to meet Teresa
I notice Becky, the crippled Barbie that I gave her last year,
the one that made her point out
Barbie's Dream House was not wheelchair-accessible,
now features red pumps and has overcome her limitations
I realize that Teresa's fate lies in the hands
of this little white girl
Briefly concerned
over the future of Latina women everywhere
until Ashley states,
"I like Teresa... she looks more like J. Lo than Barbie"

NEARLY GOD

In candlelight, I watch your Spanish eyes
staring coyly back at me
while laying naked on your bed
listening to the sounds of winds
outside South Bronx windows
shadows dancing on my olive-tanned skin
your jealous cock rises throbbing
longing to drown me
completely submerged in passion
your mother in the other room
pretending not to hear my head banging
against thin project walls
knocking knocking knocking
until our love splatters across chests and stomachs
we fall unconscious under the starry night sky
waking up the next day
to hover above you on all fours
lowering myself to the sweet intoxication
of morning breath
the taste of each other lingering in our mouths
surprising your hands with black satin sheets
tying them together to return the pleasure; the pain
your mother in the other room
pretending not to hear her baby cry
ears pressed against thin project walls
St. Therese glistening against your Nuyorican chest
while filling in that part of you
that empty space inside
revealing love with words unspoken
with every thrust

18

the image of Christ pounding against the wall
crying out my name
forcing resisting muscles to open
with every groan
taking me in
completely
with all the hunger and warmth of a third world country
two bodies one
two countries united
dos almas encadenadas
prisioneros de nuestro amor
in unholy matrimony

NEWFOUND MORALITY

Offering myself to the night
to be devoured sweetly
with hunger in my belly
    hunger in my heart
Alcohol loosening the contours of my pride
inhaling the thick smoke of a cigarette
like a roughneck of undistinguished personality
I give myself to you without price
more than just pretext or occasion
aware that life always puts frailty
in vulgar positions
Waking up the next morning
when fatigue flushes me with tenderness
that makes me horny
to allow you to penetrate me deeply
ramming it hard and calmly
marked like stigmata
Stroking myself until I discharge the most profuse joy
into the toothless mouth of Jean Genet's dead body
The motionless unclean coils of a writhing serpent
emerge from your eyes and spread to your face
as you cum inside the walls of your prison cell
to fulfill me with newfound morality

ELEGANTLY FUCKED

You fuck me while I write poetry
and the words get blurred
Worshipping my ass as if it were a Catholic deity
& after cumming deep inside of me
You run off for another cigarette
Leaving me filled with all the children we could've had

I go back to finish these poems
reveling in the thought of men
who will think of me with cocks
stiffened toward star-filled skies
reminiscing about all the nameless trade
I slept with in the last fifteen years

I want to fuck them all (up)
for making me fantasize about nipples on sweaty chests
distracting me with dicks that fill my mouth
and leave words unspoken
threesomes—being passed around like a joint

After writing a few more useless lines,
I walk out to find you passed out before me again
while jerking off in your sleep
jeans on the floor with pockets full of lint
and others digits on used napkins

Settling down was meant to end my prostitution
but poetry will always keep me out on the streets

VERBAL GRAFFITI

Dedicated to Keith Haring

It started with CHERYL BOYCE TAYLOR and BILLY FOGARTY at the Nuyorican Poets Cafe over the summer of '96. It's reading SAPPHIRE and distributing my first poetry postcards at the West Side Highway piers. It's the words of WILLIE PERDOMO. It's LATASHA NATASHA DIGGS, SARA JONES and SONJA SONG at SURF REALITY. It's reading for the first time at an open mike hosted by MATTHEW COURTNEY at BIBLIO's in Tribeca. It's going on a date with CARLO BALDI to see CARIDAD DE LA LUZ, who never showed up and entering to win my first poetry slam. It's creating the REALNESS & RHYTHMS series the third Thursday of every month at A DIFFERENT LIGHT. It's reading DOROTHY PARKER on the L train going back to Bushwick. It's mopping poetry books from the bookstore all summer and completing work on my own collection. It's MADONNA'S *BLONDE AMBITION TOUR*, PRINCE, TORI AMOS, etc. It's being called a beatnik poet and reading GINSBERG, GIORNO, and BURROUGHS for the first time. It's sharing the stage with EILEEN MYLES, PENNY ARCADE, EMILY XYZ and AL LEWIS also known as GRANDPA MUNSTER. It's not sleeping with other poets but keeping an eye out for publishers and flirting with everybody in between. It's FREEDOM OF SPEECH AND FIGHTING PREJUDICE. It's sitting with tears in my eyes on the steps of The Community Center after baring my soul with DELIVERANCE at the P.R.I.D.E. AWARDS. It's TRANCE at Meow Mix. It's *KEITH HARING'S JOURNALS*. It's JEAN MICHELE BASQUIAT paintings. It's HAL SIROWITZ AT GATHERING OF THE TRIBES AND RENT ON BROADWAY. It's listening to EDWIN TORRES at EL MUSEO DEL BARRIO not understanding a word he said.

IT'S RIDING THE SUBWAY WITH A DRUNK TISH BENSON AND A CHRIST-LIKE SAUL WILLIAMS. It's having SEX in the name of ART and creating ART to have more SEX. It's DE LA VEGA messages scribbled on the streets of New York. It's constant change and being in control, THE BEASTIE BOYS, THE BIJOU, THREE-WAY RELATIONSHIPS. IT'S CREATING THE HOUSE OF XAVIER. IT'S THE SOUND FACTORY AND JUNIOR VASQUEZ. It's an old white lady complaining to Barnes & Noble about letting a "disgusting foul-mouthed pervert" like me read at Union Square Park. IT'S LISTENING TO OTHER POETS AT THE AUDRE LORDE PROJECT IN BROOKLYN DURING A THUNDERSTORM. TALKING TO POETS. BEING A POET. It's reading a blasphemous poem at ST. MARK'S CHURCH. IT'S MEETING SUHEIR HAMMAD AND HAVING HER ASK ME IF SHE COULD BE IN THE HOUSE OF XAVIER. IT'S SOMEONE RECOGNIZING ME AS A POET WHILE DANCING IN A K-HOLE ON TOP OF A SPEAKER AT TWILO. It's looking outside the window of TENNESSEE WILLIAMS ex-lover's apartment on Central Park South. IT'S SPICE GIRLS LOLLIPOPS AND ALTOIDS. IT'S BUYING A COLLECTOR'S EDITION OF HUBERT SELBY'S *LAST EXIT TO BROOKLYN*. IT'S DREAMS OF WALKING ALONE IN THE DESERT WITH A HUGE CROSS TO BEAR. IT'S READING THE BIBLE AND WONDERING IF I AM THE ANTI-CHRIST. It's names engraved in the bathrooms of Chino-Latino restaurants. It's the graffitied walls on the Lower East Side by ANDRE CHARLES. IT'S PATTY HEARST AND THE SYMBIONESE LIBERATION ARMY. It's meeting PARKER POSEY, WILSON CRUZ and astrological diva WALTER MERCADO. It's co-starring in an independent film. IT'S JENNIFER MURPHY WINNING POET LAUREAT AT THE LOVE JONES POETRY SLAM IN FORT LAUDERDALE. It's THE GOLDEN GATE PARK AND HAIGHT STREET IN SAN

FRANCISCO. IT'S THE PHANTOM BALL AT RED ZONE. IT'S MICHAEL MUSTO'S COLUMN IN THE VILLAGE VOICE dishing it out. It's posing half-naked and leather masks. It's the sounds of *el coqui en* PUERTO RICO. It's the *cholos* y *serranos* in ECUADOR. It's students at COLUMBIA UNIVERSITY studying my work and in COLUMBIA being considered a disgrace. It's RICKY MARTIN on the cover of TIME. It's J. LO's ass. It's living my life the way I see fit. It's fuck you if you don't love me and fuck me if you do... *Y que siga... Y que siga la tradicion... bajo la luna, maybe... pero jamas en el corazon.*

IT RAINED THE DAY THEY BURIED TITO PUENTE

It rained the day they buried Tito Puente
The eyes of drug dealers following me
as I walked through the streets
past shivering prostitutes
women of every sex
young boys full of piss
and lampposts like ghosts in the night
past Jimmy the hustler boy with the really big dick
cracked out on the sidewalk
wrapped in a blanket donated by the trick
that also gave him genital herpes and Fruit Loops for breakfast
past the hospital where *Tio* Cesar got his intestines taken out
in exchange for a plastic bag where he now shits and pisses
the 40's he consumed for 50 years
past 3 of the thugs who sexually assaulted those women
at Central Park during the Puerto Rican Day parade
lost in their machismo, marijuana and *Mira mami's*
'cause *boricuas* do it better

Tito's rambunctious and unruly rhythms never touched them
never inspired them to rise above the ghetto
and, like La Bruja said, "Ghet Over It!"
his *timbales* never echoed in the salsa of their souls
though they had probably danced to his cha-cha-cha
they never listened to the message between the beats
urging them to follow their hearts

On a train back to Brooklyn
feeling dispossessed and dreamless
I look up to read one of those Poetry In Motion ads
sharing a car with somebody sleeping
realizing that inspiration is everywhere these days
& though the Mambo King's body may be six-feet under
his laughter and legend will live forever

The next morning
I heard the crow crowing, "Oye Como Va"
his song was the sunlight in my universe
& I could feel Tito's smile shining down on me

BORN THIS WAY

I want to breathe Rimbaud's last breath

I want to shower in Bukowski's golden piss

I want to wrap my legs around the sun and fuck it blind

I want to read Walt Whitman to the waves at Coney Island beach

I want to challenge the constraints of Catholics

I want to swim through Madonna's hair
        come out changed and reinvented

I want to run out to the rooftop and roll on broken glass
        lying there bloodied looking skyward

I want to foretell the future from clouds
        reaching out to touch God's naked body

I want to hang out with trannie hookers
        opening their homes and hearts as freely as their legs
        sleeping on floors surrounded by bitten off corners
        of condom packages

I want my Muse to make love to me
        pounding me hard with his hands at my wrist
        leaving me breathless and inspired to concentrate
        my faith

I want to hear him say, "I see Lorca in your eyes"

I want to love him like a little child
    troddling unafraid thru the heaven of his soul
    with whispers gone before nightfall

I want to hitchhike through the heart of America
    but the cars keep passing by

THE WORLD BEFORE ME

"You are the controller of your destiny"
-Fortune Cookie

I've been lying in darkness and contempt on a torn mattress
living in a church where I sleep with voodoo dolls
collecting the years like dust
dreaming among the dead
a glimpse of bitterness in dull eyes

I've seen death like the cock of my cousin
creeping inside coupon-paid-for diapers
stars falling silent from my eyes
until blood red roses blossomed
from the soil where his seed was planted
and the petals dripped
and the petals dripped
Fertilizing a childhood fucked in the mouth with poisons & drugs
rebellion written all over my street-streaked ass

I've been searching my soul tonight
lit only by this candlelight
slowly melting away
knocking it over to set this prison on fire
to burn down the walls that hold me hostage
the empty rooms
I smell the curly smoke
until the rebirth of wind rushes through my aging body

I still bleed on the hands that hold me down
Refuse to climb rooftops only to be pushed from grace
Taking a step back from the ledge
I've learned to move freely within my own tomb

29

BURNING DOWN THE HOUSE

Peep this . . .
From someone who once pretended to play daddy
to street kids with cunning, delinquent faces
These words are for everyone struggling in sexuality and youth-
Beware the false motives of others
and those who pretend to be brothers
Legends walking down runways like superstars
like Christ before getting nailed to the cross
Wolves wrapped in furs and sheep's clothes
Acting like they got it all
by making others feel small
(the smaller the brain, the bigger the mouth)
stealing children from their homes
luring them with falsehoods about status quo
so there will always be someone applauding
at the next ball
          always catching their falls
          always licking their balls
altar boys attending the priest's skirt
lost in a club full of treachery, jealousy, potential saints and flirts

Do not try to be what someone else thinks you should be
Define your own destiny
Achieve your own identity
love yourself and you can't fail
Plant your own seeds and watch your trees grow
If the branches get all twisted and the leaves begin to fall,
Burn down the house because this ain't no home

RISK

Emanuel, you know I love you, but I need you to be more affectionate. I don't understand why you pull away when I try to hold your hand in public? I know you love me too but it makes me feel insecure. There's nothing wrong with public displays of affection. It's important for people to see two men or two women in a loving relationship. Society will never accept us if we hide our love like there's something wrong with it. You, out of all people, should be aware of this. I mean, what are you so scared about? Do you really think I'd ever let anything happen to you?

I was six when a group of guys chased
what I thought was a girl
toward my stepfather's parked car
outside our Bushwick apartment
Lifting myself from the back seat
young and curious

Mami rolled up her window
as the young man smeared with make-up and blood
banged on the other side of the glass
crying for help
The mob caught up to him
someone pulled him by his long hair
dragged him to the hood of the car
smashing his face into the cold metal

Sometimes, I can still see his eyes
staring back at me in horror
I was introduced, for the first time,
to the words *marica* and *maricón* and faggot

It's so ironic that in your writing and performances, you come across as so revolutionary and strong, but out in public, you're so private and reserved. People look up to you and you need to take a stand. How could you get up on a stage and read the stuff you write about and then be afraid to be yourself with your lover out on the streets?

I was eleven when two men kissed outside the Manhattan store
Mami had just finished shopping in
handing her bags over to me to block my view
blocking the love
Her purchases ending up on the floor
Mami ending up on the floor
pushed out of the way by some thug
Her bags, her body, beneath me
Opening up the view
to see a group of men replacing the two previous
cursin' and punchin'
kickin' and spittin'
howlin' and laughin'
before *Mami* got up
and shoved me into her breasts to block my view
blocking the hate

Look, it's not like we have to be on top of each other everywhere we go but it would be nice to have people realize we're a couple every once and a while. It's confusing. If this relationship is going anywhere, you need to work on being more affectionate.

I want so much to touch you
fall asleep in your arms
on the back of the bus
huddling together in our own little world
where the bumps and potholes
add joy to the ride

I want to kiss you out in the open
even if it means our brutal death
because our blood will feed the cracks between the concrete
weeds will grow to remind this world that nature
will never be completely destroyed

*You've survived so much and yet you're so scared of what people
think. It doesn't make any sense at all. A real man is someone like
Stacy Amber that could live his life on a daily basis and not be
afraid to walk the streets in a tight dress and high heels.*

I was sixteen when a guy chased
what I thought was a girl
toward my trick's parked car
outside the West Side Highway piers
Lifting myself from the front seat
young and angry

33

John rolled up his window
as the young trannie smeared with make-up and blood
banged on the other side of the glass
crying for help
The guy caught up to her
before I stepped out of the car
pulled him by the hair
dragged him to the hood of the car
smashing his face into the cold metal

Sometimes, I can still see his eyes
staring back at me in horror
He was introduced, for the first time,
to the words *change* and *revolution* from a *faggot*

I just want you to be a little more affectionate. You can't keep hiding behind, "That's just the way I am." That shit don't fly with me.

I was twenty-seven when you came into my life
I had never felt more comfortable and safe
with anyone in the world
You were the first to ever challenge me
to realize that sometimes sacrifice
is the only way to salvation
to recognize that true love
requires strength and compromise
If only I had reached out
in public
to hold your hand

34 *Emanuel, you know I love you, but this isn't working out. I can't live like this. I need to be with someone who is not afraid to be themselves out in public. It's really important to me. I want to be able to kiss my lover at any given time. I need someone willing to take that risk.*

SEPTEMBER SONG

The most vivid reflection was the idea
of being on top of the world
standing higher than the clouds on one of two metal twins
far removed from religions which crumble
in the hands of ignorance
and countries where freedom of speech
is a mouth full of blood
high above the perversions and sins that held me down
feeling closest to heaven, baptized by the winds of Oyá
without much thought to the corporations below
which provided this peace

Days after towers crumble to the ground,
finally coming out of the rubble and dusting off the depression
Standing by the West Side Highway piers
where, from the distance, they once illuminated
the darkness of my loneliness
many homeless and sleepless nights out on the streets
with the hope that someday I too could reach the sky
and feel the grace of God
Through the emptiness in the skyline of my soul
and the curly smoke
I imagine those who have suffered
at the hands of oppression and hate
rising like a flock of pigeons
flying high and together in unspoken agreement

An old woman watches from across the street
something sacred behind tearful eyes
perhaps the secret to true Beauty
wearing a shawl to keep herself warm
while pacing back and forth with a fading photograph
& I realize to live as I have lived is surely absurd

Peace may not exist throughout the insanity of our world
but it can never be taken hostage from the kingdom within me
Buildings, dreams and lives may have fallen
but the walls I built around myself have also tumbled down
I still stand in a city left behind
with corporate orphans and empty beds
learning to love again
without fear and with hope for a new beginning

LOVE REMEMBERED

I was convinced you would help fulfill my American dream
After pulling myself out of the streets
and reinventing myself as a poet
all that was missing was someone to share
the pursuit of happiness

I was prepared for the picket fence or trailer park
thirsty for the promise of strength
and fortitude in the milk of your skin
but the only truth was that the whiteness consisted of cocaine

You seemed to think
that wearing the pants in the relationship
Working long hours and taking care of most of the expenses
Granting me the opportunity to challenge myself creatively
you reserved the right to stay out indulging
in drugs, sex and alcohol
sleeping with at least one of my childhood friends along the way

Perhaps you felt I deserved to be treated
like the drug dealer and prostitute I once was
my newfound self-worth and ambition
contrasting against your self-destruction and mutilation
Perhaps I was foolish to look the other way
Pretending the lonely nights would be washed away
with the passing rain
but love is not making the same mistakes
and offering the same apologies

Three years, two cats and one black eye later
It's difficult to look back at our relationship
with nostalgia and affection
Every time I miss the life we shared together
I remind myself of that weekend I stayed in bed
healing the bruises on my face
the way my mother had taught me as a child

I was wrong to think I'd get more work done without you
In your arms I dreamt again
In your eyes I came to life
Now I spend too much time crying
like you knew I would

Abandoned by one man and molested by another
In the end, we only stayed together
because I was too stubborn to admit failure and defeat
Believing your touch was my completion
when all I needed were my own hands to survive

CHILDREN OF MAGDALENE

Dedicated to Reverend Phelps

There are so many dead pretending to live amongst us now
who belong to a church hidden behind the harvest of hate
which takes us in and blinks us out with ignorant eyes
and condemn us for lying together in the tombs of our beds
while their savior hangs from nails displayed on hollow walls
and our sacrifices are left to hang on fences
bleeding rivers of glory
to wash away the sins of their world

This prejudice is the pain that clouds my eyes and knots my spine
the scars on the back of my head
engraved by those who reach out open arms
bloodied with hypocrisy, lost dreams, and intangible mantras
those who haunt our daily prayers
with the sounds of oppression
to silence our shepherds with death
because death equals dreams never to be heard of again
and our prophets get no maps to salvation

But the wind will not inherit the echoes of our souls
we will not leave our canvas with unfinished colors
or remain the uninvited children of a lesser God
we will ground our bare feet with toes in soil
listen for the wind chimes in the insanity of life
light candles for our brothers and sisters
from the West Side Highway piers of New York City
to the farm lands of Laramie, Wyoming
to the Castro Streets of San Francisco
and feel the closest we can to heaven
because true love has no boundaries
and our angels have wings too

MAGDALENA

Mami/I remember your dyed blonde hair/your milky white skin/your really bad accent/your small stature/the violent outbursts/pointing out the negatives in me/shuddering at the sound of your voice/the sound of your anger/your fist/never too far away

Your words/stabs/deep into my fatherless flesh/reminding me/always reminding me/that you were all I had/for a mother/for a father/my stepfather/your boyfriend/striking/the final blows/destroying me/as if he were my father/destroying you/as if he were your father

Mami/I remember happy times/things weren't always bad/there were times we would laugh about your leaving him/even though you'd soon take him back/they were brief lapses of happiness/before the cycle would begin again/I remember how proud you were of me/getting good grades/in spite of the abuse/even I was impressed/or was that repressed/in spite of all the pain/while you longed to be so strong/to deny your existence/the reality that we called home

I remember trips to Ecuador/Puerto Rico/Disney/Cancun/Cancun where you finally sensed something was wrong with me/that I had broken up with someone/but what was wrong with falling in love with another man/so what if he was HIV positive/so what if we had unsafe sex/so what if he was a crack addict/so what if he was cheating on me/so what/and what was wrong with then falling in love with an abusive drug dealer/what was wrong with falling in love with younger boys/older men/what was wrong with giving myself away to many men/many older men/the price was right/I needed a place to stay/you threw me out at sixteen/

the piers get cold in the winter/what was wrong with wanting to be loved/with wanting to be in love/falling in love with all the wrong men/what was wrong with that

Mami/I remember returning home several years later/ surviving the streets to reach nineteen/watching you grow tired and old/working all day at the factory/you never wante to be a welfare mom/coming home to this misery/ to throw some half-hearted dinner together/your boyfriend too old to lay a hand on me/on you/afraid to lock into the hatred in my eyes/remembering the time he fucked up and called you *Magdalena*-his mistress's name/that was the last time he laid a hand on you/the day I beat the shit out of him/the day he realized I would kill him if he *evah* touched you again/if he *evah* touched me again/ that way

I remember your stories about my real father/the one man I probably never slept with/that look in your eyes/that glow on your face/whenever you spoke of him like you really truly deeply loved him/with all your heart/before he abandoned you/these are the times I understand your anger/your wrath/your hatred toward me/not that you want to/you can't help it/it hurts/your pain/every time you look into my face/and you see him

Mami/there were good times/I know there were good times/there were great times/but my memories hold prejudices too stubborn to leave me alone

I am still a child/I can still hear your boyfriend/not my stepfather/not my father/in the kitchen/rustling about like a rat in heat/eating away at his life/belching and farting for me to hear/to hate him/to feel his presence/cringing/every time the door unlocks and he enters/I want so much for him to die/to leave us alone/to stop invading my memories/

to free me from this oppression/this white supremacy/this is my cross/my hatred toward white supremacy/not whites/supremacy/his white skin/his jokes about blacks/about *negros*/about *cholos*/about *maricones*/about *cachaperas*/ he is latino/but he is white/I am *trigueño*/I am half Puerto Rican/my real father was Puerto Rican/they are his main hatred/**those fuckin' boricuas/those fuckin' jibaros**/he swears he is white/he can pass/yet his heart is darker than any skin/I want so much for him to die

Mami/I want to write you a happy poem/a loving poem/ dedicate it to you/with all my heart and soul/but I can't Mami/it is Mother's Day/all I can think about is this pain/ all I can think about is the last man that hurt me/all I know is anger/it is where everything comes from/every time I fall in love/I am reminded of this anger/it is my solace/it is my comfort/it is my peace/it is my strength in letting go

I reach out to touch my boyfriend/he pulls away/I ask to be held/he refuses/remains guarded/I share with him my story/he tells me I need therapy/pulls the sheets away from me/I fall asleep/wake up frozen/he is gone/gone to be with his *Magdalena*

AL PIE DE OYÁ

I shared a drink with Miguel Algarin,
founder of the Nuyorican Poets Cafe,
the place that sanctified me from the streets with poetry

& I found myself thinking about Mikey,
not the Mikey X I had contrived as an alias in my writings,
but the Miguel Piñero that had been this man's best friend

Miguel (Algarin) stared back at me as if to compare
& I remembered one of his poems which read
"Instructions for ceremony should be written as a poem"

When I die, I want to be burned with my books
flesh and words melting into one (*echame candela*)
ashes unleashed over the West Side Highway piers
gently dispersed by the winds of Oyá
carrying my soul to the secret verses and hidden places
where the children will always find me
where my lovers will always find me
where I had found me watching the bright lights of New York City
hoping one day I would shine as bright as the stars
inspiring hope in the hearts of hustlers to come

However, with many nights spent stretched out on her graves
tombstones casting shadows on faded wings
the Queen of Cemeteries will want to embrace me
If buried, black is sanctioned
color of my children and eyes and revolutions
garnish me with poetry and rosaries to set the spirit on fire
haunting dreams with words and deliverance

43

And so maybe I proved prostitutes can become poets
shamelessly rising above and beyond homelessness
Sitting there like a novelist posing in lush, spacious apartments
while French journalists covered me with cigarette mist
asking questions like, "What does 'munchin' trade' mean?"

I came a long way only to find that it wasn't enough
that the mistakes of the past limit the future
even though when it rains, we all get wet-
the prostitute, the poet, the prophet
Each breath brings me closer to the end of this journey
until dead is dead is dead

In the end, it doesn't matter how I lived,
how I died, or what becomes of what is left
Listen for me in the flicker of candles

Inspiration often comes from silence

LOOK ON DOWN FROM THE BRIDGE

When I was little, my mother made me wash my face
with the water used to soak rice before cooking
Abuela told her this would get rid of my freckles
Throughout childhood,
she would buy me lotions and creams
with the hopes that the constellations on my face
the last remainders of my other heritage
would disappear in the night leaving nothing but
darkness

Years later, *Mami* caught me caressing the boy next door
the one that told me freckles gave me character
She slammed the door on my fingers leaving them purple blue
Unaware that someday I would use them to share this story

These are the realms and auras
of dreams and death and discovery and disappointment
which inspire words to flare like a challenge dance
before the ink stains fade

If I keep these secrets locked inside
set myself apart
I will corrode with loneliness
grow old, wither and die
a moth alone in a dark closet

Each has a story to be told and retold
long after the theater lights go off
memories will still seep from veins leading toward hands
that will share stories about pain and healing
because, though the truth sometimes hurts,
it is always beautiful

WICKED SMILE

I feel introspective
the need to distance myself from all this madness
the insanity of my life
struggling to reach the top
only to find that it means nothing at all
that true happiness lies within myself
that this anger needs to be absolved before I can move on
that in denying you the words that need to be said
I only imprison myself
this loneliness- self-imposed
but before I free myself from these chains
before I race against the wind
I will ground myself firmly
feel Mother Earth caress my callused feet

confront this pain which was your gift
with the knowledge that it was predestined
by a God which still exists
through your wicked laughter fading from tarot cards
I will pick up the pieces to mend my heart
fight to be strong
to look unscathed in front of the audience
to challenge you with the indifference that was your charm
And though I only miss your need for me
your hunger to feast on my confidence
This new poem I write for you
this new candle I light to produce images of my soul
this need for attention
walking away revealed from every stage
means nothing more than words brought together
to vaguely express this feeling of loss
to walk this bridge over emptiness
but your smile keeps haunting me like a vengeance

MARICÓNA

Dedicated to Jeanette Colon

At least you died in the winter
when I could feature black softly woven sweaters
contrasting against the diamond glints on snow
which supposedly represent reflections of your soul

Outside, the cold cold air does not compare
to the temperature of your skin
the last time I caressed your hair back
while you slept in your coffin
You always kept it short and sexy... *bien chuchi*
to compliment the cute stubble on your chin
the peach fuzz you were proud to grow
like the bodega boys and *tecatos*
I would blow on the down low
in exchange for a pack of smokes and a dime bag

It's fucked up they couldn't get you a new heart
After giving yours away so freely many times
Even the strap you used to hide your breasts
couldn't hold back your heart from jumping out
everytime a fly *mamasita* passed you by

Hanging out with you made me feel real butch
Spending life like it was borrowed money
Smoking blunts and playing handball
throughout Bushwick courts
Downing '40's at Orchard Beach out in the Boogie Down Bronx
which you dubbed *Chocha* Beach with a wink and a smile
Shopping for boxers, tanktops,
the latest ghetto gear to pass for hardcore hoodies

You didn't laugh when I told you I secretly wrote poems
dreamt of falling in love with someone who would do me right
wanted to settle down someday and adopt two cats
You even gave me a copy of *Stone Butch Blues* for inspiration
though I never had the chance to tell you that it made me cry
the same tears I tried to hold back
throughout life and at your funeral
like raindrops on the edge of a roof

If peace is the freedom to express yourself completely
without fear of repercussion or hate
the courage to seek out the kingdom within yourself
without apology or regret,
then you were always resting in peace

I put on the Sean John winter hat you stole
from that butch named Buddy
head out to Astroland to spill beer
from a bottle on the concrete ground
feeding the *muertos* like you taught me
Maricóna, I will always be riding front seat, hands in air,
on the Coney Island Cyclone with you

PIER QUEEN FOR HIRE

HUSTLER

WORK EXPERIENCE
Highly competitive retail environment, location scouting for
customer satisfaction, blow jobs, training potential hustlers,
using men to locate finances, distributing STD's, protecting
territory from competition, penetration, menage-a-trois

REASONS FOR LEAVING
Age limitations, adversity with Latino Fan Club

REFERENCES
Tri-State area, Jennifer Blowdryer

DRUG DEALER

WORK EXPERIENCE
Securing space at major NYC nightclubs to conduct business,
purchase ordering substances, accessories and business
attire, packaging and distribution, handling publicity and
promotions while maintaining low profile from police force,
pricing, counting large sums of money, advising consumers
on proper use of purchases, delivery services

REASONS FOR LEAVING
Mayor Giuliani, improved quality of life, too much drama
involved within club scene, high competition and quick
turnaround rate, closing of Sound Factory

REFERENCES
New York Police Department

SKILLS
Knowledge of current street terminology used for drugs and sex, knowledge of sexually transmitted diseases, handling of high powered weapons, recognizing undercover cops, highly experienced in proper application of lubrication devices and use of condoms

COÑO! CARAJO! PUÑETA! CARAY!

COÑO!
I'm tired of homoboys from the projects
Stab wounds and stretch marks
Surviving with scrambled egg sandwiches and a cup of coffee-
light and sweet—in the morning
Cruising the mami chula's while checking out the papi chulo's
The only pussy in their existence-
Anheuser's Busch and a couple of cats
Never standing up for a gay cause
'Cause fucking and getting sucked off by men
Does not make them faggots... just horny
Living on the D-L
Missing letters- E-N-I-A... as in DENIAL

CARAJO!
I'm tired of dating fag rag queens
Looking to be seen with me because
I'm supposedly a minor downtown celebrity writer
Mouthing off stories over dinner
As if I should be nostalgic over childhood experiences not my own
Hoping someday to end up in one of my poems
Well, here's a fuckin' line for you-

51

PUÑETA!
I'm tired of self-loathing homosexuals and hypocrite religions
threatened by openly gay men
that are sexually active, happy and healthy
Feeling we should all be repressed or dying
condemning gay couples for wanting to adopt
Picketing outside pride events
with signs that read, "God Hates Fags"
while shoving cocks full of cum in the openings of children

CARAY!
I'm tired of being hispanically indeterminate
A little bit of Ecuador and a little bit of Puerto Rico
makes me look a little Mexican
Therefore, never considered a true Nuyorican
100% of nothing, except *Maricón*
Displaced and dismissed for being an openly gay writer
In English and Spanish, the word 'homosexual' is spelled the same
Limiting conversation in both languages
I too could claim to be bisexual-
buy me something and I'll get sexual
I too could claim to be straight-
hiding behind the skirts of latin machismo
I too could mainstream my story
and rewrite my ending to sell my own bodega dreams

CORPORATE ORPHAN

Clockin' in the hours
takes up most of my life
Staring at the watch
killing time dead
dead like office equipment souls
by painting my nails with white-out
playing with rubber band balls
adjusting my chair
getting high on Magic Markers
sneaking personal phone calls
engraving my name onto the desk
jamming the photocopy machines
while waiting for something to happen
besides secret meetings by the water cooler-
frowned upon socializing

I keep our picture in an empty Altoids tin
inside temporarily borrowed drawers
frozen smiles ripped from the pages of a fag rag
reminding me of another forthcoming weekend
to lose myself on the dance floor
underneath disco balls instead of fluorescent lights

This job is just money in my pocket
Time spent in parentheses
Creative energy lost in cubicles

but writing this poem at this temp gig
is like trying to swim down the chainsmoking supervisor's throat

AMERICANO

I look at myself in the mirror
trying to figure out what makes me an American
I see Ecuador and Puerto Rico

I see brujo spirits moving across the backs of Santeros
splattered with the red blood of sacrificed chickens
on their virgin white clothes and blue beads for Yemaya
practicing religions without a roof

I see my own blood
reddening the white sheets of a stranger
proud American blue jean labels on the side of the bed

I see Don Rosario in his guayabera
sitting outside the bodega
with his Puerto Rican flag
reading time in the eyes of alley cats

I see my mother trying to be more
like Marilyn Monroe than Julia De Burgos
I see myself trying to be more
like James Dean than Federico Garcia Lorca

I see Carlos Santana, Gloria Estefan,
Ricky Martin and Jennifer Lopez
More than just sporadic Latin explosions
More like fireworks on el Cuatro de Julio
as American as Bruce Springsteen, Janis Joplin,
Elvis Presley and Aretha Franklin

I see Taco Bells and chicken fajitas at McDonald's
I see purple, blue, green, yellow and orange
I see Chita Rivera on Broadway

I am as American as lemon merengue pie
as American as Wonder Woman's panties
as American as Madonna's bra
as American as the Quinteñeros, the Abduls, the Lees,
the Jacksons, the Kennedys
all immigrants to this soil
since none sound American Indian to me
as American as television snow after the anthem is played
and I am not ashamed

Jose, can you see...
I pledge allegiance
to this country 'tis of me
land of dreams and opportunity
land of proud detergent names and commercialism
land of corporations

If I can win gold medals at the Olympics
sign my life away to die for the United States
No small-town hick is gonna tell me I ain't an American
because I can spic in two languages
coño carajo y fuck you

This is my country too
where those who do not believe in freedom and diversity
are the ones who need to get the hell out

PAPI CHULO

When I look into your *papi chulo* eyes
I see happiness and joy
the Christ-child *con los tres reyes magos*
& bags full of toys
for the first time noticing
the beauty of brightly lit *bodegas*
against cobalt skies
the subway smiles of homeless mothers
watching two men kiss quick secret goodbyes
walking away from each other
banjee boys on their way home
forbidden love glistening in their souls
like the melted candles and whispered prayers
from altars glowing late at night
in the *barrios* of a sleepless city
-still prejudiced and cold

When I touch your *papi chulo* skin
I abandon myself to ecstasy and hope
childhood scars lost somewhere in your embrace
abrasando tus sueños wrapped inside my coat
your breath *acariciandome* like the soft island breezes of Oyá
soothing the jagged edges of my ghetto face
while gently rocking under the moonlight back and forth
back and forth
back and forth
to the rhythms of salsa and Spanish lullabies
engraved in memory like graffitied names on a hostel wall

When I kiss your *papi chulo* lips
I close my eyes to taste your tropics
my inhibitions drowning in the sweet river of your saliva
struggling to survive somewhere deep within
while tongues dance to the beat of our hearts
deseando que estos momentos would last forever
in a world without boundaries
in love without limits
en la isla de Nueva York
papito lindo
tu amor
es mi bendición

CAFÉ CON LECHE

Mi cuerpo café
junto a tu piel de leche
despierta en mi mil sueños
mientras beso tus labios dulces
para darte todo mi calor
Perdido en tus bellos ojos verdes
aunque no me entiendes
con estas palabras te quiero enamorar
Mi corazón te lo entrego sin precaución
porque eres mi alma
y he esperado toda mi vida
para encontrarte en mi camino
y saber con solo una sonrisa
que eres mi angel
y que este amor no es traición
por tu sexo o color
no importa lo que diga la gente
ahora solo importa tú y yo

JIBARO DREAMS

En la isla de Nueva York
I search for secret gardens
spiritual sanctuaries
a child lost in a forest of *Jibaro* dreams
where *santos* sail through the *salsa* of my soul
& only fruits fallen from the tree
violently smashing against once rat-infested grounds
remind me of the outside world
sweet juices spilling
feeding the soil
with *abuela's lagrimas*
fathering life to our culture
nature to our concrete jungle
Earth bathing in virgin nectars
lodging seeds in uncemented wombs
struggling for growth somewhere beneath
the choking tight clothes of buildings and overpopulation
outside verandah fortresses
Spanish lullabies and *guaguanco* healing her birth
amongst the *casitas de nuestra gente*
still standing
defiantly
freedom from oppression
paradise
amidst metal and decay

JE T'AIME

I fell in love with New Orleans
lost in the eyes of a French boy
tu as de beaux yeux
green as a forest of dreams
reflections of the Riviera in the iris of his ghost
smile as bright as the fires of burning ships
his lips caressing me with warm winds
discovering me like a rag doll
found amidst an abandoned village lost to the revolution

My heart submerged like an entire city with just one kiss
no cares in the world other than waking up in his embrace
whispering *tu as de beaux yeux* like a voodoo spell in my ear
praying to the dead that this life would last forever
where painters capture the hearts of poets
where masks disguise the decadence of free spirits
where southern bells inspire the symphony of the soul
where the only sacrifice is a harlequin tear and a melting candle

I fell in love with New Orleans with just one phrase
tu as de beaux yeux
Now the rosaries of my religion
are replaced with Mardi Gras beads

ALEXIS & SABLE

Silly to admit you are my muses
neutered boys with *Dynasty* drag queen names
sunning on the windowsill
stalking power line pigeons
while listening to jazz all day
waiting for me to come home
to scattered pictures of two divas in every possible pose
welcoming me with heartbroken meows

Hairy husbands sharing my bed for mutual cat naps
indulging in your sweet kitty kisses and morning bites
heavenly creatures jealous of anything requiring more attention
than the complete trust of a furry belly offered for indulgence
stealing pens to keep me from writing

No longer giveaway kittens
huddled in a soggy cardboard box
Licks from your tongue heal like Jesus
the perfect purr—the greatest pleasure
reason to survive in a dog eat dog world

SINGLE

I stare at you from the dance floor
Imagining the lyrics playing are for me alone
nothing worth reciting to the beaches
in the dreams where we walk together hand-in-hand
grooves like waves crashing
drowning this delusional desire
of another place in the world for us

All I have to offer are a few lines without a repetitive hook
hoping to catch your eyes
piercing through the smoke-filled darkness
singling me out in a room full of half-naked bodies
to complete this groove
This would have been a great song
an original with no need to be remixed for momentary pleasure

Thank you for putting my name on your list
You should have heard the poem
I recited under the blaring music
seen the way my body swayed to your rhythms

By the time you notice me from the dee-jay booth
I will have smoked my last cigarette
used up all my complimentary drink tickets
left you to sample your next record
as I head to Coney Island to catch the sun rise

LATIN GIRL

You are the ones with the brown cocoa skin,
the milky white flesh, *la piel de morenita*
the Spanish eyes and the wicked smiles
With hands on your *cinturas* featuring finely polished nails
Amongst yourselves, the loud exaggerated laughter
echoing defiantly from the back of the bus

You enjoy the sweet taste of lollipops
and the rebellious look that chewing
fantastical pieces of bubblegum
leaves imprinted on your *quinceñera* face
popping and snapping until the teacher finishes talking
about whatever he or she is talking about

You are the ones with overcrowded closets
jewels glistening brightly like lip gloss against your innocence
with secret diaries and heart-stamped journals
hidden underneath pillowed beds
jotting down memories of your youth
which will ignite your passion somewhere down the road
inspire the humble words of poets
and the songs you croon to on the radio

Boyfriends — entertaining yet unnecessary
like your vast collection of *muñecas* and stuffed animals
which decorate your poster-wallpapered rooms
a trail of broken hearts held tight
until you meet the right one,
the one who respects and truly loves you
the one who doesn't treat you like his property
offering you his hand in marriage
to wipe away *abuela's lagrimas*
after a long struggle for independence
from the oppression of old-fashioned *machismo*

When I see one of you with a baby carriage
my heart breaks
flooded by the memories of my once teenage mom
and the hell I've put her through

You will grow up to fuss even more about your make up
fidgeting over pints of ice cream and pastries
which will leave you with Mami's or Titi's legendary hips,
hips that are hip to the Latin culture
on women who age gracefully if unknowingly
while religiously watching favorite *telenovelas*

Mira nena...
Never lose the beauty of your spirit
never forget your freedom to pursue your dreams
for that freedom no longer belongs to men alone

Sigue soñando...

DUE TO AN UNFORTUNATE LADY

The little woman wrote honestly even if poorly
dropping casual and vain profanities
to keep herself from falling apart like a ten cent toy
while *educated* poets doubling as critics
yap yap yapped their assholes off
making her feel like a mongrel

It wasn't enough that she abandoned everything to follow it
sharing insults and lunch at notorious round tables
attempting suicide at least four times to remain full of wit

I wrote passionately even if badly
publishing untrained and raw words
to keep myself from selling my body like a fifty dollar toy
while *academic* poets doubling as experts
blah blah blahed their assholes off
making me feel like a bum

But holding your breath around the homeless
does not mean they do not exist
I don't care to be called a *partial artist*
avoiding every course and degree imaginable
to remain full of charm

Poetry is no longer just for the privileged elite
truth is no longer celebrated by the masses
or saluted by the enemy
Still, poets from all backgrounds
continue to write what they feel and see
even if their words do not come across as eloquently

If the little woman were still alive today
I would tell her how she inspired me
to live my life over again
making the same inexcusable mistakes
walking down the same empty streets of my soul
burning a bridge a day
because regret is self-destructive

VERBAL GRAFFITI 2

It's JOYCE JONES ON PERCUSSION. It's passing the blunt and deep conversations on the stoop. It's having other poets walk around quoting, "YO, MIRIAM, THROW DOWN THE BABY." It's understanding religion. IT'S SOMEONE WHISPERING "FAGGOT." IT'S POETS DEGRADING PERFORMANCE POETS AS "NOT REALLY" POETS. It's not reading anything but REAL POETRY all summer. It's poetic "prose." It's reading between the lines. It's making a decision for yourself. It's rhythms and syllables and words. IT'S WORDS UNSAID. Traditions, culture, spirituality, time. IT'S DRAMA! IT'S THE PAST MANIFESTING ITSELF IN MY PRESENT AS I WORK TOWARDS THE FUTURE. It's MIGUEL PIÑERO at the Naropa Institute in Boulder, Colorado. It's feeling inspired and inspiring others. REVOLUTION-EVOLUTION-PEACE-FREEDOM. It's PRINCESS WALKING RUNWAY. IT'S WILLI NINJA VOGUING. IT'S BETTE DAVIS AND JOAN CRAWFORD FILMS IN BLACK AND WHITE. It's the BRONX ZOO. It's reading FITZGERALD'S *THE GREAT GATSBY* IN A SOUTH AMERICAN BEACH AND IN BROOKLYN LIVING OFF ARROZ CON HABICHUELAS Y GHETTO JUICE. IT'S PEDRO ALMODOVAR FILMS. It's cruising pieces at the piers. IT'S CONVERSATIONS OVER THE INTERNET WITH JUSTIN CHIN, WHO'S "NOT BITTER JUST DESCRIPTIVE." IT'S BEING ON THE CAFE CON LECHE FLOAT FOR GAY PRIDE. IT'S "THE PHILLY, THE PHILLY, THE PHILLY, THE BLUNT." It's wearing all black once a year to protest police brutality. IT'S PAMELA SNEED asking me to read at NEW NEUTRAL ZONE. It's touching the lives of gay and lesbian youth. IT'S PERFORMING "CHELSEA QUEEN" AT DUMBA WITH BILLY AND CARLOS DOLLS AT GAY SHAME. It's everything that goes around comes around. IT'S PICKING UP THE POETRY CALENDAR TO FIND OUT

WHEN THE HELL I'M READING. IT'S THE INSANITY OF MY LIFE. IT'S POETRY IN MOTION. IT'S A BOOK CALLED *PIER QUEEN*. It's acknowledging my strengths and weaknesses yet having the audacity to self-publish the book anyways. It's a vicious review in THE NEW YORK BLADE. It's watching other poets get too big for their own britches and keeping a distance. It's running into the drug dealers you used to work for and giving them an autographed copy of your book. IT'S HARLEM IN THE SUMMER. It's *BASKETBALL DIARIES*. IT'S THE BOYS AT KINKO'S. IT'S JULEE CRUISE'S "INTO THE NIGHT." IT'S PASSIONATE SEX WITH SOMEONE YOU LOVE. IT'S FALLING IN LOVE. IT'S EXPRESSING ANGER AND PAIN AND LETTING IT GO. IT'S MOVING ON. IT'S SPIRITUAL GROWTH. IT'S BEAUTY IN DARKNESS. IT'S WORDS THAT DON'T RHYME. IT'S ART. IT'S POETRY. IT'S KEEPING IT REAL. IT'S SPRAY-PAINTED IMAGES TAGGED FOREVER IN MY SOUL.

REVOLUTIONARY SOUL

As the largest growing minority in the United States
living within the raw deals of this American dream
this American dream which rapes and abuses our resources
distorts our histories
We, the ones at the bottom rung of recognition
at the highest level of criticism
We the Nuyoricans, Caribbeans,
the Central Americans, the South Americans
must unite beyond differences
beyond color lines
beyond the *bodegas*
our move must take shape
our strengths must be gathered
con nuestros pueblos en el corazon
because only *solidaridad* is our salvation
against racism, prejudice and self-destruction
against the old-fashioned traditions of latin *machismo*
with pencil-thin mustaches
whose pants have quickly fallen
We must put an end to the stereo-typical belief
that we are gun-crazed, welfare-cheating,
$200 sneaker-wearing, promiscuous bastards
We cannot afford to run away from ourselves
abandoning our brothers and sisters
carrying them away dead with candles glowing
because when you hide your reality like the sun behind clouds
en el silencio nocturno
you will still see the project lights in the distance
you will still hear the Spanish babies cry
you will still witness the murder of Anthony Baez
you will still feel the presence of our ancestors
pounding dirt roads with sandals
you will still feel the presence of our ancestors

in the Yoruba breezes which perfume these ghettos
and twilight will still creep through your soul
You see, denial of our culture
is in the circle of the supremacist eye
which watches us repress one another
while *abuelo's lagrimas* fall from forgotten balconies
I have learned that the biggest threat I pose to this society
is to be young, latino and ambitious
even with thoughts that do not walk in straight lines
The century of blood *de mi gente*
this mixed blood which pumps through these latin veins
calls upon me to set them free
to take control of my life
no longer a colonial subject
no longer scratching defiance onto the back of strangers
The future is near

the revolution is here
a revolution without fear
to create our own change
to reconstruct ourselves
let our voices bounce from every wall and city
to the frenzied *ritmos y sueños* clattering within our hearts
let us crowd into this photograph
take color fading snapshots of oppression
and move forward
with pride

BABY BLUE

We met at a lesbian rock concert at CBGB's
introduced by the slick of a guitar and strained vocal chords
When we first kissed outside your police car it took me by surprise
I pulled away with a single tear full of hope
from the same eye that ended the last relationship black and blue
Maybe you weren't aware I had seen you before
thought to myself, "That's the kind of man I want to be with"
Not because you were comfortable up on the rally stage
adored by so many in the crowd brought together by pride
Not because of the strength and courage of your NYPD uniform
showing the world we identify
with more than just sex while inspiring fantasies
but because I never imagined to be so deserving
I found myself struggling with the contradiction of that kiss
Failed relationships had slowly destroyed
the hopeless romantic in me
And with just a smile you challenged that fear of love
Traveling different paths to get where we were
life is poetry that way
when the prostitute and the police officer
share a fragile moment worth heaven
Arrest me in your arms again and set this spirit free

UNDONE

Criticized for ambition
crucified for success
and yet every time I reach a new peak
I see another mountain I want to climb
Surviving the streets as a hustler
does not mean I have to spread my ass cheeks
wide open for publication
open the gates of banjee heaven for profiles or reviews
throw my legs high up in the raw air
until I can touch the grace of God with my callused feet
or prostitute my prose by pounding my peers with slam poetry
I will not humor you with verse about apology or regret
I will not stand before you and pretend to be a visionary bard
I will not memorize my lines to impress you
with passion and strength
I will not punctuate each word to show clarity and depth
I will not define myself as a humble spiritual activist poet
pretending not to want your attention
because I am far too complex to be anything close to simple
and far too scarred to be your warrior without pain
I give voice to my experiences without shame
emotionally crippled enough to turn to others for love
Yet, Amiri Baraka once wrote that the word 'love'
spelled backwards is 'e-v-o-l' pronounced "evil"
I wonder if Amiri knew that adding 'u-t-i-o-n' to that
would give us 'evolution' and tongues untied
Sarah Jones once wrote,
"your revolution will not happen between these thighs,
your revolution will not happen between these thighs"
and the revolution will not happen between my legs
but evolution will continue to grow inside this womb
until I birth this rage inside of me
drenched in prose and fed by poetry

fathered by poverty and the richness of reality
this child will be born with blood smeared on bookshelves
and his or her name shall be Art
It will have many verbal brothers and sisters
because this whore from the piers
this queen self-crowned
has yet to whisper in many more ears
with verses that are yet to come
from a kingdom fortressed by five nails
with which I scratch and crawl
engrave my name in history
clench my fist
tattoo the letters 'l-o-v-e' on my knuckles
to fight for this poetry in my heart
I am not done fighting yet
I am not done reading yet
I am not done writing yet
the future is in our words

About the Author:

Emanuel Xavier is also the author of a poetry collection, *Pier Queen*, and the novel, *Christ-Like*. He currently lives in New York.

Emanuel Xavier Management:
Shifty Entertainment, Inc.
336 West 17th Street, Suite 2C
New York, NY 10011-5059
Tel/Fax: 212-741-2062

About the Cover Designer/Photographer:

Boston-based designer/photographer/writer/consultant/ fuckup Shane Luitjens brings a wide range of experience to his work, including award-winning interactive design for Monster.com and Drugstore.com as well as founding and directing HOOK, the nation's only harm reduction publication by, for, and about male sexworkers (www.hookonline.org). He is also the poetry editor for *suspect thoughts: a journal of subversive writing*. For further information on writing and photography, surf to www.lethalwhitetrash.com. For further information on design, point and click to www.torquere.com. Joy everyday.

About Suspect Thoughts Press:

Suspect Thoughts Press is a terrible infant hell-bent
to publish challenging, provocative, stimulating,
and dangerous books by contemporary authors
and poets exploring social, political,
queer, and sexual themes.

suspect thoughts press
www.suspectthoughts.com